FAST AND FURIOUS

Tick
Tock

www.hachette.co.uk

First published in the USA in 2013 by TickTock, an imprint of Octopus Publishing
Group Ltd
Endeavour House
189 Shaftesbury Avenue
London
WC2H 8JY
www.octopusbooks.co.uk
www.octopusbooksusa.com

Distributed in the US by
Hachette Book Group USA
237 Park Avenue
New York NY 10017, USA

Distributed in Canada by
Canadian Manda Group
165 Dufferin Street
Toronto, Ontario, Canada M6K 3H6

ISBN 978-1-84898-733-3

Printed and bound in China

Picture credits:
b=bottom; c=center; t=top; r=right; l=left

Alamy 75t, 85t; Aviation Picture Library: 12-15, 20-21, 24-27; Beken of Cowes
76-77c, 80-81c; Car Photo Library – carphoto.co.uk 6, 40-69; Bill Scott 84-85c;
Corbis 30-31, 81t, 90-91c; Hawkes Ocean Technologies 91t; iStockphoto.com
28-29; Jane's Defence Weekly 88-89c; John Clark Photography 72-73;
Lockheed 7t, 18-19; Nasa 8-11, 22-23; RNLI 7b, 78-79, 86-87; Shutterstock front
cover, 1, 38-39; Skyscan 16-17; Stena 74-75c; US Coast Guard 32-35, 89t

Every effort has been made to trace the copyright holders, and we apologize
in advance for any unintentional omissions. We would be pleased to insert the
appropriate acknowledgments in any subsequent edition of this publication.

Contents

Introduction

Fast and Furious showcases some of the fastest and most powerful vehicles ever made, in three thrilling sections: In the Air, On Land, and On the Water.

In the Air

Discover the most impressive aircraft of the past 50 years, from the Space Shuttle, entrusted with 135 missions, to top-secret military planes like the Lockheed SR-71 Blackbird and the stealth bomber B2-Spirit. Plus commercial jetliners like the legendary Concorde and the Airbus A380 that can carry nearly 1,000 passengers.

On Land

Marvel at the most phenomenal cars and bikes ever built, including classic vehicles unsurpassed in speed and design. Find out about the Aston Martin V12 Vanquish,

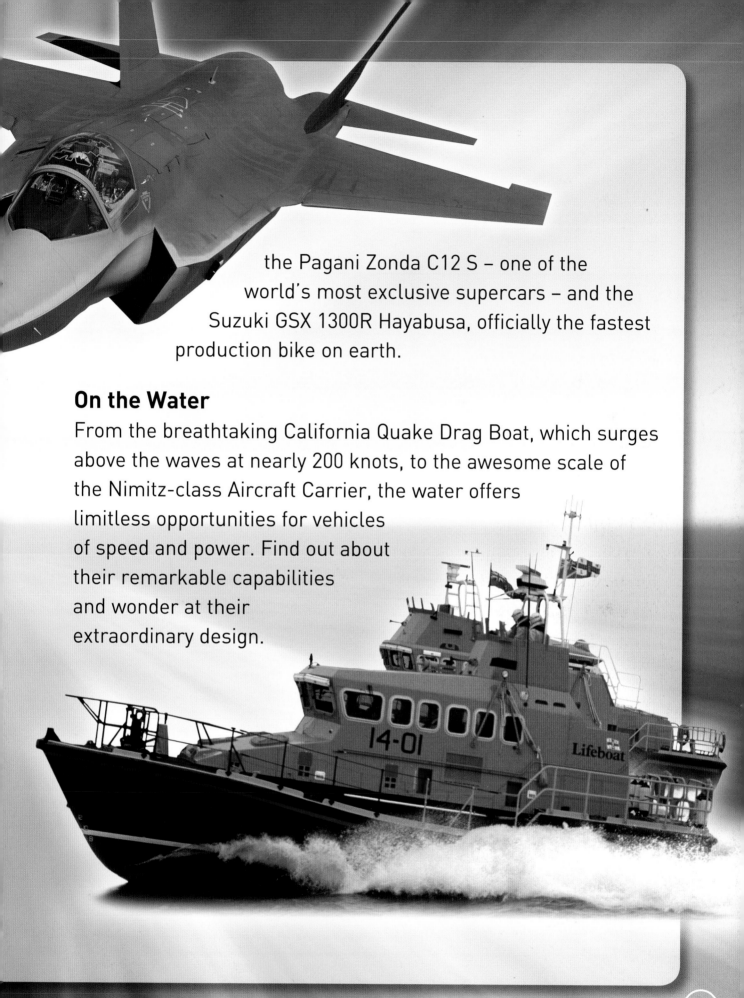

the Pagani Zonda C12 S – one of the world's most exclusive supercars – and the Suzuki GSX 1300R Hayabusa, officially the fastest production bike on earth.

On the Water

From the breathtaking California Quake Drag Boat, which surges above the waves at nearly 200 knots, to the awesome scale of the Nimitz-class Aircraft Carrier, the water offers limitless opportunities for vehicles of speed and power. Find out about their remarkable capabilities and wonder at their extraordinary design.

14-01

Lifeboat

In the Air

This section is dedicated to every type of aircraft, from the Space Shuttle, the first real spacecraft to be brought back to Earth, to military planes, like the monster eight-engine B-52 Stratofortress – the fighter pilots' "Big Ugly Fat Fellow" – which will keep flying at least until 2040. Then there is the iconic, streamlined, and superfast Concorde, which was once the world's fastest passenger jetliner, and vital rescue craft like the P-3 Orion Firefighting Airtanker and the Jayhawk helicopter, whose speed and power are essential for emergency intervention and to assist those stranded at sea.

F-117A Nighthawk

First flown in 1981, the F-117A might be the weirdest aircraft ever made. Its shape was designed to break up enemy radar signals. Because it could be refueled in midair, the F-117A was able to fly almost anywhere. Retired in 2008, this amazing plane was made by the US company Lockheed.

Three Nighthawks are on display in the US. At the United States Air Force Museum visitors can walk right up to this incredible aircraft.

DID YOU KNOW?
Nighthawk pilots called themselves "Bandits."

26

DID YOU KNOW?

Stacks of brilliant facts to really impress your friends! For example, did you know that as the X-43A reaches supersonic speeds, some of its metal parts melt from the intense heat? And there's more...

The F-117A was a bomber plane. Its zigzag-shaped doors opened and shut very quickly to release bombs.

The hundreds of flat surfaces on the plane made it almost invisible on radar.

STATS & FACTS

LAUNCHED: 1981

RETIRED: 2008

ORIGIN: US

MODELS: 5 PROTOTYPES AND 59 PRODUCTION AIRCRAFT

ENGINES: 2 GENERAL ELECTRIC F404-F1D2 TURBOFANS, EACH GIVING 10,800 LB (4,899 KG) THRUST

WINGSPAN: 43 FT 4 IN (13.2 M)

LENGTH: 65 FT 11 IN (20.08 M)

COCKPIT CREW: 1

MAXIMUM SPEED: MACH 1 (617 MPH/993 KM/H)

MAXIMUM WEIGHT: 26.25 TONS (23.8 METRIC TONS)

RANGE: WITHOUT AIR REFUELING, ABOUT 1,500 MILES (2,400 KM)

LOAD: 2 LASER-GUIDED BOMBS

COST: $42.6 MILLION

(27)

STATS & FACTS

All key data at your fingertips, to help you compare military aircraft and commercial jetliners: from launch date, model, and range to top speed, weight, wingspan, crew, and passenger capacity. See which is the fastest and which the most powerful!

Space Shuttle

Early space flights relied on rockets—giant tubes fired into orbit. The Space Shuttle was the first spacecraft that could be brought back to Earth. NASA used it on 135 missions from 1981 to 2011, when it was retired.

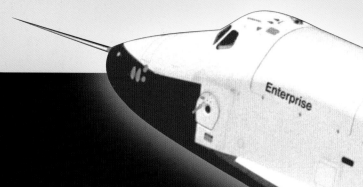

The front area houses 10 crew members, including two pilots. In the middle is a large bay for satellites. At the back are three big rocket engines.

DID YOU KNOW?

The Shuttle's boosters fall off into the ocean. They are recovered and used again.

Heat-resistant tiles protect the Shuttle when it returns to Earth. It glides onto a runway and is slowed down by a big parachute.

The orbiter is attached to a huge tank holding liquid oxygen and liquid hydrogen. A solid rocket booster is on each side.

STATS & FACTS

LAUNCHED: 1981

ORIGIN: US

MODELS: DISCOVERY, ATLANTIS, ENDEAVOUR, COLUMBIA, CHALLENGER

ENGINES: 3 ORBITER ENGINES THAT EACH PRODUCE A VACUUM THRUST OF 470,000 LB (213,188 KG)

WINGSPAN: 78 FT (23.79 M)

LENGTH: 122 FT (37.24 M)

CREW: UP TO 10

MAXIMUM SPEED: 17,500 MPH (28,164 KM/H)

MAXIMUM LANDING WEIGHT: 110 TONS (100 METRIC TONS)

RANGE: 116–403 MILES (187–143 KM)

LOAD: SATELLITES, COMPONENTS FOR THE JOINT SPACE STATION, AND SPACE EXPERIMENTS

COST: $1.7 BILLION, PLUS $450 MILLION FOR EACH LAUNCH

X-43A

NASA (National Aeronautics and Space Administration) is best known for space exploration, but it also conducts important research into aircraft. The X-43A is one of the latest research planes. It is a hypersonic (faster than Mach 5) plane that flies without a pilot.

Guinness World Records recognized the X-43A scramjet with a world speed record for a jet-powered aircraft—an amazing Mach 9.6!

NASA 1

DID YOU KNOW?

At high Mach speeds the heat is so great that metal portions of the plane's frame melt.

The X-43A's first flight took place on June 2, 2001. It was dropped from a B-52 over the Pacific Ocean. However, the plane broke up in the sky.

The X-43A has a wide bottom, flat top, and two fins. Its scramjet engine burns hydrogen-based fuel.

STATS & FACTS

LAUNCHED: 2001 (TEST VERSION)

ORIGIN: US

MODELS: X-43A, X-43B, X-43C, X-43D

ENGINE: GASL HYDROGEN-FUELED SCRAMJET ENGINE

WINGSPAN: 5 FT 2 IN (1.5 M)

LENGTH: 12 FT 1 IN (3.66 M)

CREW: UNMANNED AT PRESENT

MAXIMUM SPEED: MACH 10 (6,600 MPH/10,622 KM/H)

MAXIMUM WEIGHT: 1.4 TONS (1.3 METRIC TONS)

RANGE: UNKNOWN

COST: $250 MILLION

SR-71 Blackbird

In 1960, the Soviet Union shot down an American spy plane. After this disaster the US government hired Lockheed Corporation to build a craft that would never be shot down. The result was the amazing SR-71, packed with cameras and sensors. Despite its dangerous missions, not one of the 32 Blackbirds built was lost in combat.

Nicknamed "Blackbird" because of its dark color, the plane is made of titanium alloy, which protects it from the extreme heat produced by flying at Mach 3.

DID YOU KNOW?

The SR-71 flight manual contains over 1,000 pages and is available online.

The Blackbird was top secret. President Lyndon Johnson didn't even admit it existed until six month after its maiden flight.

Large spikes keep the plane balanced.

STATS & FACTS

LAUNCHED: 1966

RETIRED: 1998

ORIGIN: US

MODELS: SR-71A, SR-71B; OTHER VARIANTS INCLUDE THE A-12, YF-12A, M-21, AND D-21 DRONE

ENGINES: 2 PRATT & WHITNEY J58-P-10S WITH AFTERBURNERS

WINGSPAN: 55 FT 6 IN (16.94 M)

LENGTH: 107 FT 5 IN (31.65 M)

COCKPIT CREW: 2

MAXIMUM SPEED: MACH 3 (2,200 MPH/3,500 KM/H)

MAXIMUM WEIGHT: 70 TONS (64 METRIC TONS)

RANGE: 3,300 MILES (5,400 KM)

LOAD: SENSORS AND CAMERAS

COST: $33 MILLION TO BUILD; $50,000 AN HOUR TO FLY

Eurofighter Typhoon

Four European countries—Germany, Italy, Spain, and the UK—developed this warplane together. Typhoons are built on four separate assembly lines, with each country building its own national aircraft.

Only 15 percent of the Eurofighter's body is metal. The rest is mainly lightweight carbon fiber, which keeps the plane from overheating.

DID YOU KNOW?

By January 2011, Typhoons in service since 2003 had flown over 100,000 hours.

The twin engines allow the Typhoon to accelerate to Mach 1—the speed of sound—in under 30 seconds. The Typhoon also takes off in just five seconds!

The Typhoon has a large triangular wing and small powered foreplanes on each side of the nose.

STATS & FACTS

LAUNCHED: 2002

ORIGIN: EUROPE

MODELS: TWIN-ENGINE, CANARD-DELTA WING MULTIROLE AIRCRAFT ENGINES: 2 EUROJET EJ200 REHEATED TURBOFANS EACH PROVIDING 20,000 LB (9,072 KG) THRUST

WINGSPAN: 35 FT 11 IN (10.95 M)

LENGTH: 52 FT 5 IN (15.96 M)

COCKPIT CREW: 1 OR 2

MAXIMUM SPEED: MACH 2 (1,550 MPH/2,495 KM/H)

MAXIMUM WEIGHT: 26 TONS (23.5 METRIC TONS)

RANGE: 1,800 MILES (2,900 KM)

LOAD: GUNS, MISSILES, BOMBS

COST: $104 MILLION

The Concorde

In 1962, Britain and France joined forces to build a supersonic commercial airplane—the Concorde. First flown in 1969, the Concorde entered service in 1976 and flew for 27 years before being retired. Cruising at Mach 2—twice the speed of sound—this amazing plane made the trip from London to New York in just over three hours.

The Concorde's slim body and paper-dart shape enabled it to fly more than twice as fast as other passenger planes.

DID YOU KNOW?

Twenty Concordes were built. Five are now on show in museums.

The Concorde's entire nose hinged down so the pilot could see when landing.

The Concorde's four powerful engines allowed the plane to reach 225 mph (363 km/h) in just 30 seconds.

LAUNCHED: 1969

ORIGIN: FRANCE AND THE UK

MODELS: ONLY 1 PRODUCTION TYPE, WHICH IS LARGER THAN PROTOTYPES

ENGINES: 4 ROLLS-ROYCE/SNECMA OLYMPUS S93 TURBOJETS, PROVIDING 38,000 LB (17,260 KG) THRUST

WINGSPAN: 83 FT 10 IN (25.6 M)

LENGTH: 202 FT 4 IN (61.66 M)

COCKPIT CREW: 2

MAXIMUM SPEED: MACH 2 (1,350 MPH/2,173 KM/H)

MAXIMUM WEIGHT: 204 TONS (185 METRIC TONS)

RANGE: 4,500 MILES (7,242 KM)

LOAD: ROOM FOR 140 PASSENGERS, BUT USUALLY SEATED 100

COST: $46 MILLION (IN 1977); THIS WOULD BE ABOUT $350 MILLION TODAY

Joint Strike Fighter

In 1995, the US Air Force and US Navy launched a program for a JSF (Joint Strike Fighter). The goal was to produce the next generation of planes for airfields and aircraft carriers.

All JSFs carry weapons on each side of the fuselage.

DID YOU KNOW?

The JSF will replace fighter, strike, and ground attack aircraft for the US, UK, Canada, Australia, and their allies.

There are three versions of the JSF. The F-35A is the basic version. The F-35B has a more powerful engine. The F-35C (right) has a bigger wing, which can fold.

The rear exhaust produces thrust to lift the aircraft.

STATS & FACTS

LAUNCHED: 1995

ORIGIN: US

MODELS: F-35A, F-35B, AND F-35C

ENGINES: 1 PRATT & WHITNEY F135 TURBOFAN OR 1 F136 GE TURBOFAN; FOR THE F-35B, 1 F135 PRATT & WHITNEY TURBOFAN OR 1 F136 GE TURBOFAN AND ROLLS-ROYCE ALLISON ENGINE-DRIVEN LIFT FAN, DELIVERING 25,000 LB (11, 340 KG) AND 18,000 LB (8,164 KG) THRUST

WINGSPAN: UP TO 43 FT (13.1 M)

LENGTH: UP TO 51 FT 5 IN (15.5 M)

COCKPIT CREW: 1

MAXIMUM SPEED: MACH 1.8 (1,200 MPH/1,900 KM/H)

MAXIMUM WEIGHT: 25 TONS (22.7 METRIC TONS)

RANGE: ABOUT 1,380 MILES (2,200 KM)

LOAD: ENORMOUS VARIETY OF GUNS, MISSILES, AND BOMBS

COST: $92 MILLION

Harrier

By the late 1950s, air forces wanted planes that could operate from parking lots, forest clearings, or even small ships. Hawker Aircraft in the UK launched one of the first VTOL (Vertical Takeoff and Landing) aircraft in 1969. This plane is the Harrier. It is also known as the "Jump Jet."

DID YOU KNOW?

The US Marine Corps uses the Harrier to provide air power for forces invading an enemy shore.

This single-seat Sea Harrier operates from aircraft carriers. There are also two-seater and training versions.

Harriers have a system called VIFF (Vectoring in Forward Flight) that lets them perform tricky maneuvers.

STATS & FACTS

LAUNCHED: 1969

ORIGIN: UK

MODELS: 11 VERSIONS

ENGINES: 1 ROLLS-ROYCE PEGASUS 6 OR 11, DEPENDING ON THE VERSION; THE VECTORED THRUST TURBOFAN PROVIDES 15,000 LB (6,800 KG) TO 23,500 LB (10,660 KG) THRUST, DEPENDING ON THE VERSION

WINGSPAN: UP TO 30 FT 4 IN (9.25 M)

LENGTH: UP TO 47 FT 8 IN (14.5 M)

COCKPIT CREW: 1 TO 2

MAXIMUM SPEED: MACH 1 (735 MPH/1,180 KM/H)

MAXIMUM WEIGHT: UP TO 15.5 TONS (14 METRIC TONS)

RANGE: WITHOUT AIR REFUELING, ABOUT 1,700 MILES (2,736 KM)

LOAD: MISSILES, ROCKETS, BOMBS

COST: $24 TO $30 MILLION

The engine has two nozzles on each side. They blast downward for takeoff and forward to slow down.

B-52 Stratofortress

After World War II, the US Air Force built B-52s—monster eight-engined jet bombers. In 1952, the first of these giants took flight. Still flying and fighting, they will be in service until at least 2040. Today's pilots say that the last B-52 pilot has not yet been born.

Fighter pilots refer to the B-52 as "BUFF": Big Ugly Fat Fellow.

Sensors enable the plane to fly close to the ground during combat missions.

DID YOU KNOW?

The B-52 has six ejection seats.

Air refueling makes it possible for B-52s to fly almost anywhere in the world.

STATS & FACTS

LAUNCHED: 1952

ORIGIN: US

MODELS: B-52A TO B-52H

ENGINES: 8 PRATT & WHITNEY TF-33 TURBOFAN ENGINES

WINGSPAN: 185 FT (56.4 M)

LENGTH: 159 FT 4 IN (49 M)

COCKPIT CREW: 6

MAXIMUM SPEED: 650 MPH (1,046 KM/H)

MAXIMUM WEIGHT: 244 TONS (221 METRIC TONS)

RANGE: 8,800 MILES (14,160 KM)

LOAD: NUCLEAR OR HIGH-EXPLOSIVE BOMBS, CRUISE MISSILES, AND A VARIETY OF GUNS

COST: $9.29 MILLION (IN 1955)

B-2 Spirit

Stealth airplanes are designed to avoid detection by enemy radar. First flown in 1989, the B-2 stealth bomber looks like it came from another planet.

B-2 technology comes at a price—each plane costs an amazing $1.16 billion!

The strange bulges in the B-2 hide its engines, cockpit, and bombs.

DID YOU KNOW?

The B-2's skin is jet-black and smooth and all joints are hidden.

The plane has just two crew members: a pilot and a mission commander. The rest of the cockpit contains computer-controlled flight equipment.

STATS & FACTS

LAUNCHED: 1989

ORIGIN: US

MODELS: THE US AIR FORCE HAS 20 PLANES, ALL SLIGHTLY DIFFERENT

ENGINES: 4 GENERAL ELECTRIC F118-GE-100 ENGINES, EACH WITH A THRUST OF 17,300 LB (7,850 KG)

WINGSPAN: 172 FT (52 M)

LENGTH: 69 FT (21 M)

COCKPIT CREW: 2

MAXIMUM SPEED: HIGH SUBSONIC

MAXIMUM WEIGHT: 200 TONS (181 METRIC TONS)

RANGE: INTERCONTINENTAL

LOAD: CONVENTIONAL OR NUCLEAR WEAPONS

COST: $1.16 BILLION

F-117A Nighthawk

First flown in 1981, the F-117A might be the weirdest aircraft ever made. Its shape was designed to break up enemy radar signals. Because it could be refueled in midair, the F-117A was able to fly almost anywhere. Retired in 2008, this amazing plane was made by the US company Lockheed.

Three Nighthawks are on display in the US. At the United States Air Force Museum visitors can walk right up to this incredible aircraft.

DID YOU KNOW?

Nighthawk pilots called themselves "Bandits."

The F-117A was a bomber plane. Its zigzag-shaped doors opened and shut very quickly to release bombs.

The hundreds of flat surfaces on the plane made it almost invisible on radar.

STATS & FACTS

LAUNCHED: 1981

RETIRED: 2008

ORIGIN: US

MODELS: 5 PROTOTYPES AND 59 PRODUCTION AIRCRAFT

ENGINES: 2 GENERAL ELECTRIC F404-F1D2 TURBOFANS, EACH GIVING 10,800 LB (4,899 KG) THRUST

WINGSPAN: 43 FT 4 IN (13.2 M)

LENGTH: 65 FT 11 IN (20.08 M)

COCKPIT CREW: 1

MAXIMUM SPEED: MACH 1 (617 MPH/993 KM/H)

MAXIMUM WEIGHT: 26.25 TONS (23.8 METRIC TONS)

RANGE: WITHOUT AIR REFUELING, ABOUT 1,500 MILES (2,400 KM)

LOAD: 2 LASER-GUIDED BOMBS

COST: $42.6 MILLION

Boeing 787 Dreamliner

The 787 Dreamliner is the first midsized commercial airplane able to fly long-range routes. Launched in 2004, but in service since 2011, the Dreamliner incorporates breatkthrough technologies that make it 20 percent more fuel efficient than airplanes of the same size.

The 787 has a smooth nose shape.

DID YOU KNOW?

The 787 is equipped with systems that report its maintenance requirements directly to ground-based computers.

The larger 787-9 can carry up to 290 passengers on routes of 9,800 miles (15,750 km).

The four-panel windscreen and large windows offer a good view of the horizon.

The cabin windows on the 787 are the largest of any commercial airplane and use "smart glass" that dims automatically. No blinds are needed!

STATS & FACTS

LAUNCHED: 2004

ORIGIN: US

MODELS: 787-8, 787-9

ENGINES: 2 GENERAL ELECTRIC OR ROLLS ROYCE ENGINES

WINGSPAN: 197 FT (60 M)

LENGTH: UP TO 206 FT 5 IN (63 M)

COCKPIT CREW: 2

CRUISING SPEED: MACH 0.85 (647 MPH/1,041 KM/H)

MAXIMUM TAKEOFF WEIGHT: 272 TONS (247 METRIC TONS)

RANGE: 9,800 MILES (15,750 KM)

LOAD: UP TO 290 PASSENGERS

COST: $193 TO 228 MILLION

Airbus A380

Ever since the first plane took to the skies, aircraft have gotten bigger and bigger. In 2007, European manufacturer Airbus introduced the largest commercial aircraft to date: the enormous Airbus A380.

This gentle giant is the quietest wide-body jetliner in the air. It generates 50 percent less noise than its nearest competitor.

DID YOU KNOW?

During takeoff the wings of the A380 flex upward by over 13 feet (4 meters).

The double-decker A380 can carry up to 853 passengers.

The A380 includes open spaces and social areas. The interiors can be custom-designed. Singapore Airlines' A380s include separate sitting and sleeping areas, complete with full-sized beds!

STATS & FACTS

LAUNCHED: 2007

ORIGIN: EUROPE (SPECIFICALLY FRANCE, GERMANY, SPAIN, AND THE UK)

MODELS: A380-800 PASSENGER PLANE; A380-800F FOR CARGO

ENGINES: 2 NEW-GENERATION ENGINE OPTIONS: THE ENGINE ALLIANCE GP7200 AND ROLLS-ROYCE TRENT 900

WINGSPAN: 261 FT 10 IN (79.8 M)

LENGTH: 238 FT 8 IN (72.75 M)

COCKPIT CREW: 2

SEATING: UP TO 853

MAXIMUM SPEED: 588 MPH (945 KM/H)

MAXIMUM WEIGHT: 625 TONS (569 METRIC TONS) FOR TAKEOFF

RANGE: 9,200 MILES (14,800 KM)

LOAD: UP TO 853 PASSENGERS OR 165 TONS (150 METRIC TONS) OF CARGO

COST: ABOUT $250 MILLION

P-3 Orion Firefighting Airtanker

P-3 Airtankers are old military aircraft that were originally developed as spy planes. They were adapted for civilian use and are now used to fight forest fires. They carry massive amounts of fire retardant, which is dropped on the blaze below.

DID YOU KNOW?

The Orion is named after a group of stars called Orion, the Great Hunter.

The P-3 used for firefighting has low wings and four turbine engines with four-blade propellers.

Computer-controlled doors under the body of the plane open to drop the retardant.

The fire retardant is dropped in a line, which acts as a barrier to stop the fire from speading.

STATS & FACTS

LAUNCHED (AS AIRTANKER): 1990

ORIGIN: US

MAXIMUM POWER: 2,500 BHP

LENGTH: 116 FT 9 IN (35.6 M)

WINGSPAN: NEARLY 100 FT (30 M)

HEIGHT: 38 FT 9 IN (11.8 M)

MAXIMUM SPEED: 411 MPH (657 KM/H)

RETARDANT TANK CAPACITY: 3,000 GALLONS (11,356 LITERS)

MAXIMUM LOAD: 22 TONS (20 METRIC TONS)

WEIGHT: 48 TONS (43.4 METRIC TONS)

MAXIMUM TAKEOFF WEIGHT: 70 TONS (63.4 METRIC TONS)

TAKEOFF RUN REQUIRED: 4,265 FT (1,300 M)

CREW: 15

HH-60J Jayhawk

Air-sea rescue helicopters are used to save people stranded at sea. The HH-60J Jayhawk is employed by the US Coast Guard. In 2015, all 42 HH-60J helicopters will be updated. The new aircraft will be renamed the MH-60T.

DID YOU KNOW?

The Jayhawk is based on the VS-300 helicopter, developed by Russian-born American engineer Igor Sikorsky. The VS-300 first flew in 1939.

A satellite navigation system is used to find people in need of help. The pilot holds the helicopter in place while a rescuer is lowered by winch.

The small tail rotor stops the helicopter from spinning around and keeps it perfectly balanced.

The rotor blades can be folded if the helicopter needs to be stored or transported.

STATS & FACTS

LAUNCHED: 1986

ORIGIN: US

MAXIMUM POWER: 2 X 1,800 BHP

LENGTH: 65 FT (19.81 M)

ROTOR DIAMETER: 54 FT (16.46 M)

HEIGHT: 17 FT (5.18 M)

CRUISE SPEED: 160 MPH (258 KM/H)

MAXIMUM SPEED: 300 MPH (483 KM/H)

FUEL CAPACITY: 590 GALLONS (2,233 LITERS)

MAXIMUM LOAD: 3.7 TONS (3.4 METRIC TONS)

WEIGHT: 6.7 TONS (6.1 METRIC TONS)

RANGE: 700 MILES (1,127 KM)

SURVIVOR CAPACITY: 6 PERSON

CREW: 4

On Land

The swiftest, most powerful and iconic two- and four-wheel vehicles ever to hit the road are the stars of this section. They're classic, stylish, but most of all fast! Marvel at the elegant Bugatti Veyron 16.4, which could fly off the tarmac at 250 mph (400 km/h) if it weren't for the clever Formula One aerodynamics, or the rather unique $1 million McLaren F1, with its distinctive butterfly doors and central driving position. No less impressive are the "king of all sports bikes," the Ninja ZX-14, which, with its 1,441 cc engine, is the most powerful production bike ever, and the Suzuki GSX 1300R Hayabusa, officially the fastest bike on earth!

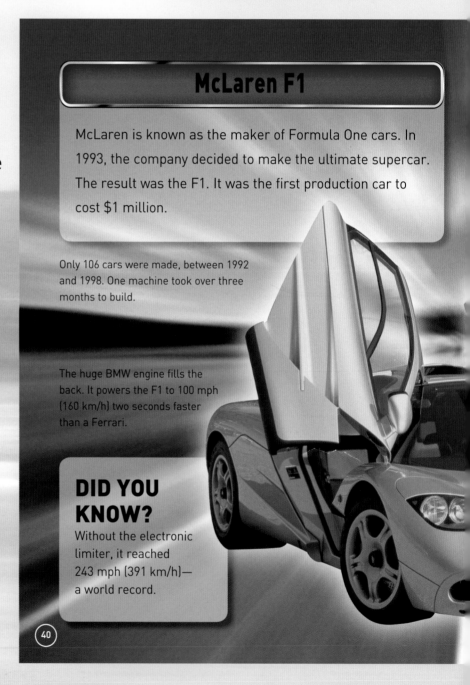

McLaren F1

McLaren is known as the maker of Formula One cars. In 1993, the company decided to make the ultimate supercar. The result was the F1. It was the first production car to cost $1 million.

Only 106 cars were made, between 1992 and 1998. One machine took over three months to build.

The huge BMW engine fills the back. It powers the F1 to 100 mph (160 km/h) two seconds faster than a Ferrari.

DID YOU KNOW?
Without the electronic limiter, it reached 243 mph (391 km/h)—a world record.

40

DID YOU KNOW?

Mine these nuggets of knowledge to give you the edge over your friends! Who would have guessed that a turbocharged Blackbird could do a wheelie at 200 mph (320 km/h) or that buying a Pagani Zonda entitled you to a free pair of driving shoes, made by the Pope's shoemaker! It doesn't get more exclusive than that!

The central driving position is unusual for a sports car. So are the two rear seats.

And there's more...

STATS & FACTS

All key data at your fingertips, to help you compare engine size, power, torque, speed, and acceleration of the best cars and bikes on land, and discover which is the fastest and which the most powerful! Buckle up, rev up, and feel the power!

STATS & FACTS

LAUNCHED: 1993

ORIGIN: UK

ENGINE: 6,064 CC 48-VALVE V12, MIDMOUNTED

MAXIMUM POWER: 627 BHP AT 7,400 RPM

MAXIMUM TORQUE: 479 LB PER FT (649 NM) AT 7,000 RPM

MAXIMUM SPEED: 240 MPH (386 KM/H)

ACCELERATION:
0–60 MPH (100 KM/H) IN 3.2 SECONDS
0–100 MPH (160 KM/H) IN 6.3 SECONDS

WEIGHT: 1.25 TONS (1.14 METRIC TONS)

COST: $1 MILLION

41

Bugatti Veyron 16.4

Volkswagen bought the legendary brand Bugatti in 1998 and launched the Veyron in 2003. A new model was produced in 2005. Inspired by the old Bugattis, it featured F1 safety technology so that the car could safely top 250 mph (400 km/h). It is so fast it would lift off the ground if it weren't for the clever aerodynamics.

DID YOU KNOW?

A special edition Veyron 16.4 was created in collaboration with the fashion house Hermès. Unveiled at the 2008 Geneva Motor Show, it is so special it costs $2.26 million!

Ceramic brakes stop the car faster than it accelerates. It stops in 2.3 seconds from 60 mph (100km/h)!

The interior of the Bugatti Veyron 16.4 had to feel elegant, luxurious, and classic, while featuring the most modern technology.

To be fast, the Veyron 16.4 must be light. It is made from the lowest weight materials, including titanium, carbon, and aluminum.

STATS & FACTS

LAUNCHED: 2005

ORIGIN: FRANCE

ENGINE: 8.0L W16-CYLINDER, QUAD TURBOCHARGER

MAXIMUM POWER: 1,001 BHP (736 KW)

MAXIMUM TORQUE: 1,922 LB PER FT (1,250 NM) AT 2,200–5,500 RPM

MAXIMUM SPEED: 253 MPH (407 KM/H)

ACCELERATION: 0–60 MPH (0–100 KM/H) IN 2.5 SECONDS

WEIGHT: 4,162 LB (1,888 KG)

COST: $1,700,000 (BASIC PRICE)

McLaren F1

McLaren is known as the maker of Formula One cars. In 1993, the company decided to make the ultimate supercar. The result was the F1. It was the first production car to cost $1 million.

Only 106 cars were made, between 1992 and 1998. One machine took over three months to build.

The huge BMW engine fills the back. It powers the F1 to 100 mph (160 km/h) two seconds faster than a Ferrari.

DID YOU KNOW?

Without the electronic limiter, it reached 243 mph (391 km/h)— a world record.

The central driving position is unusual for a sports car. So are the two rear seats.

STATS & FACTS

LAUNCHED: 1993

ORIGIN: UK

ENGINE: 6,064 CC 48-VALVE V12, MIDMOUNTED

MAXIMUM POWER: 627 BHP AT 7,400 RPM

MAXIMUM TORQUE: 479 LB PER FT (649 NM) AT 7,000 RPM

MAXIMUM SPEED: 240 MPH (386 KM/H)

ACCELERATION:
0–60 MPH (100 KM/H) IN 3.2 SECONDS
0–100 MPH (160 KM/H) IN 6.3 SECONDS

WEIGHT: 1.25 TONS (1.14 METRIC TONS)

COST: $1 MILLION

Pagani Zonda C12 S

This car was designed by Horacio Pagani, who is from Argentina. It is named after a wind that blows from the Andes Mountains. The Pagani Zonda is perhaps the most exclusive supercar. Approximately 25 Zondas are built per year.

This C12 S model has a massive V12 engine.

If you drive a Zonda, you have to travel light. The car doesn't have a trunk!

DID YOU KNOW?

When you buy a Zonda, you get a pair of driving shoes made by the Pope's shoemaker.

The Zonda looks like a fighter plane. It has a glass-roofed cabin and twin spoilers. The inside is made of aluminum, suede, leather, and carbon fiber.

STATS & FACTS

LAUNCHED: 2001

ORIGIN: ITALY

ENGINE: 7,010 CC V12, MIDMOUNTED

MAXIMUM POWER: 562 BHP AT 5,500 RPM

MAXIMUM TORQUE: 553 LB PER FT (750 NM) AT 4,100 RPM

MAXIMUM SPEED: 220 MPH (354 KM/H)

ACCELERATION: 0–60 MPH (0–100 KM/H) IN 3.7 SECONDS

WEIGHT: 1.38 TONS (1.25 METRIC TONS)

COST: $500,000

Jaguar XJ220S

In the late 1980s, British carmaker Jaguar built a supercar called the XJ220. The car was delivered in 1992 and its price was $580,000. Two years later, Jaguar produced a faster, lighter, and cheaper version, the XJ220S.

The spoiler stretched across one of the widest sports cars ever made.

DID YOU KNOW?

In 1994, race-car driver Martin Brundle reached 217 mph (347 km/h) in an XJ220S—at the time a record for a production car.

The XJ220S was built by TWR (Tom Walkinshaw Racing). The design was based on the XJ220C cars that took part in the Le Mans race in France in 1993.

STATS & FACTS

LAUNCHED: 1992

ORIGIN: UK

ENGINE: 3,498 CC TWIN-TURBO V6, MIDMOUNTED

MAXIMUM POWER: 680 BHP AT 7,200 RPM

MAXIMUM TORQUE: 527 LB PER FT (715 NM) AT 5,000 RPM

MAXIMUM SPEED: 217 MPH (350 KM/H)

ACCELERATION: 0–60 MPH (0–100 KM/H) IN 3.3 SECONDS

WEIGHT: 1.19 TONS (1.08 METRIC TONS)

COST: $580,000

The XJ220's aluminum body was replaced with carbon fiber to make the XJ220S even lighter.

Lamborghini Murciélago

Ferruccio Lamborghini was a wealthy Italian tractor maker. Unhappy with his Ferrari, he decided to build a better car. In 1966, Lamborghini made the first supercar, the Miura. In 2001, the company introduced the Murciélago. Production of the Murciélago ended in 2010. Its successor, the Aventador, was released in 2011.

DID YOU KNOW?

The Lamborghini logo is a charging bull. The Murciélago was named after a bull that fought so well in a bullring in Spain that its life was spared.

To reverse the Murciélago, most drivers flip open a door and sit on the edge of the car so they can look over their shoulders!

The roof and the doors of the Murciélago are made of steel. The rest of the car is made of carbon fiber.

The Murciélago has four-wheel drive and a safety system that slows the car down if it starts to lose its grip on the road.

STATS & FACTS

LAUNCHED: 2001

ORIGIN: ITALY

ENGINE: 6,192 CC V12, MIDMOUNTED

MAXIMUM POWER: 571 BHP AT 7,500 RPM

MAXIMUM TORQUE: 479 LB PER FT (649 NM) AT 5,400 RPM

MAXIMUM SPEED: 205 MPH (330 KM/H)

ACCELERATION: 0–60 MPH (0–100 KM/H) IN 4 SECONDS

WEIGHT: 182 TONS (1.65 METRIC TONS)

COST: FROM $350,000

Ferrari F50

Ferrari makes some of the finest sports cars in the world. The F50 is one of the most exclusive models ever built. Just 349 cars were produced, between 1995 and 1997, to celebrate the Italian legend's 50th anniversary. This incredible car boasted a slightly less powerful version of a 1989 Formula One engine.

DID YOU KNOW?

The F50 was very expensive. But you still had to roll the windows up and down by hand!

TPV 16

Underneath the car, the body is completely flat. The four exhausts stick out through holes cut into the rear, just like a race car.

The F50's body, doors, and seats are made from lightweight carbon fiber.

The engine is in the middle of the F50. It powers the Ferrari to 60 mph (100 km/h) in under four seconds.

STATS & FACTS

LAUNCHED: 1995

ORIGIN: ITALY

ENGINE: 4,699 CC 60-VALVE V12, MIDMOUNTED

MAXIMUM POWER: 520 BHP AT 8,500 RPM

MAXIMUM TORQUE: 347 LB PER FT (471 NM) AT 6,500 RPM

MAXIMUM SPEED: 202 MPH (325 KM/H)

ACCELERATION: 0–60 MPH (0–100 KM/H) IN 3.7 SECONDS

WEIGHT: 1.36 TONS (1.23 METRIC TONS)

COST: AROUND $500,000

Porsche 911 GT2

From the outside the GT2 looks like an ordinary Porsche 911 Turbo. But inside all of the luxuries have been removed to make it run like a race car. The car has harder suspension, a roll cage, special brakes, and lots of extra power!

DID YOU KNOW?

A GTS RS variant went on sale in 2010. It could top 205 mph (330 km/h). Only 500 cars were available in the US, and they sold out within hours.

The GT2 is 10 percent more powerful and 7 percent lighter than the 911 Turbo.

The spoiler and side panels have vents that cool the huge engine. There are also slats in the hood.

The GT2 accelerates to 186 mph (298 km/h) and brakes to a stop in less than 60 seconds.

STATS & FACTS

LAUNCHED: 2001

ORIGIN: GERMANY

ENGINE: 3,600 CC 24-VALVE TURBO FLAT 6, REAR-MOUNTED

MAXIMUM POWER: 455 BHP AT 5,700 RPM

MAXIMUM TORQUE: 459 LB PER FT (622 NM) AT 3,500 RPM

MAXIMUM SPEED: 197 MPH (317 KM/H)

ACCELERATION: 0–62 MPH (0–100 KM/H) IN 4.1 SECONDS

WEIGHT: 1.6 TONS (1.44 METRIC TONS)

COST: $245,000

Aston Martin V12 Vanquish

British carmaker Aston Martin made its first sports car in 1914. Nearly 90 years later, the V12 Vanquish went on sale. Made from 2002 until 2006, it had a powerful engine and a body made of lightweight aluminum and carbon fiber. It was one of the fastest cars in the world.

DID YOU KNOW?

Superspy James Bond drove a V12 Vanquish in the movie *Die Another Day*. 007's car had rockets, guns, and an ejection seat.

The V12 was built with Formula One–style gearshift paddles behind the steering wheel.

Body panels were shaped by hand. The V12 Vanquish is popular with car collectors.

Monster 19-inch (47.5-cm) wheels and high-performance tires gripped the road.

STATS & FACTS

LAUNCHED: 2002

ORIGIN: UK

ENGINE: 5,935 CC V12, FRONT-MOUNTED

MAXIMUM POWER: 460 BHP AT 6,500 RPM

MAXIMUM TORQUE: 400 LB PER FT (540 NM) AT 5,500 RPM

MAXIMUM SPEED: 190 MPH (306 KM/H)

ACCELERATION: 0–60 MPH (0–100 KM/H) IN 4.5 SECONDS

WEIGHT: 2 TONS (1.83 METRIC TONS)

COST: $250,000

TVR Tuscan

The TVR Tuscan is a sports car that was manufactured in the United Kingdom from 2000 to 2006. The car was made as light as possible and had a huge engine. As a result, it was amazingly fast and cost less than its rivals.

DID YOU KNOW?

John Travolta drove a purple Tuscan in the 2001 movie *Swordfish*.

To get into the Tuscan, drivers pressed a button under the sideview mirror. To get out, they twisted a knob in the car.

The roof and rear window could be removed and stored in the trunk. There was even space left over for suitcases!

The engine filled most of the space under the hood.

STATS & FACTS

LAUNCHED: 2000

ORIGIN: UK

ENGINE: 3,605 CC 24 VALVE INLINE 6, FRONT-MOUNTED

MAXIMUM POWER: 350 BHP AT 7,200 RPM

MAXIMUM TORQUE: 290 LB PER FT (393 NM) AT 5,500 RPM

MAXIMUM SPEED: 180 MPH (290 KM/H)

ACCELERATION: 0–60 MPH: (0–100 KM/H) IN 4.4 SECONDS

WEIGHT: 1.2 TONS (1.1 METRIC TONS)

COST: $77,000

Kawasaki Ninja ZX-12R

The Japanese company Kawasaki has always made very fast motorcycles. Produced from 2000 to 2006, the ZX-12R was one of the fastest bikes on the planet, capable of just under 200 mph (320 km/h). The Ninja also had a big fuel tank, so it could travel long distances.

The ZX-12R could go from 70 mph (113 km/h) to a complete stop in under four seconds.

DID YOU KNOW?

The ZX-12R had the widest back tire of any sports bike. It was a huge 8 inches (20 cm) wide!

The scoop under the headlight forced air into the engine, which dragged extra fuel in. This gave the ZX-12R even more power.

In 2012, the "king of all sports bikes" was launched. With an 87.9 cubic inch (1,441 cc) engine, the Ninja ZX-14 is the most powerful production bike ever made.

STATS & FACTS

LAUNCHED: 2000

ORIGIN: JAPAN

ENGINE: 73.2 CU IN (1,199 CC)

CYLINDERS: 4

MAXIMUM POWER: 165 BHP AT 9,800 RPM

MAXIMUM TORQUE: 2.7 LB PER SQ FT (130 NM) AT 7,800

GEARS: 6

DRY WEIGHT: 463 LB (210 KG)

MAXIMUM SPEED: 190 MPH (305.8 KM/H)

FUEL TANK CAPACITY: 5.3 GALLONS (20 LITERS)

COLORS: BLACK/GOLD, SILVER, KAWASAKI GREEN

COST: $15,021

Suzuki GSX 1300R Hayabusa

The Japanese manufacturer Suzuki was founded in 1952. In 1998, it built a new motorcycle called the Hayabusa. In 2000, the speed of all new bikes was limited by law. This model is officially the fastest production bike on Earth, since no other motorcycle can be made to go faster without being altered.

The British Land Speed Record for a motorcycle is held by a turbocharged Hayabusa. It topped 241 mph (388 km/h)!

DID YOU KNOW?

A Hayabusa is so powerful that it can wear out a back tire in as little as 1,000 miles (1,600 km).

This is the Hayabusa 2011. Powered by a 1,340 cc, 16-valve engine, it is one of the fastest sports bikes currently in production.

The Hayabusa is a bird of prey that eats blackbirds. Suzuki named its new bike Hayabusa because it is faster and more powerful than Honda's Blackbird.

STATS & FACTS

LAUNCHED: 1998

ORIGIN: JAPAN

ENGINE: 79.2 CU IN (1,298 CC)

CYLINDERS: 4

MAXIMUM POWER: 155 BHP AT 9,000 RPM

MAXIMUM TORQUE: 2.8 LB PER SQ FT (134 NM) AT 6,800 RPM

GEARS: 6

DRY WEIGHT: 474 LB (215 KG)

MAX SPEED: 186 MPH (299 KM/H)

FUEL TANK CAPACITY: 4.7 GALLONS (18 LITERS)

COLORS: BLUE & BLACK, BLUE & SILVER, SILVER

COST: $13,327

Ducati 999S

Ducati is an Italian motorcycle company that was bought by the German car manufacturer Audi in 2012. The 999 was the fastest and most expensive motorcycle Ducati produced. It was made of carbon fiber and aluminum.

The seat and fuel tank could be moved backward and forward, and the footrests moved up and down. This Ducati was comfortable to ride, whatever your height.

DID YOU KNOW?

The Ducati 999S was capable of reaching 62 mph (100 km/h) in under three seconds.

This is the Ducati 1199 Panigale. The name links the bike to its origins in Borgo Panigale, near Bologna, Italy. The area is called "Motor Valley."

The 999 range enjoyed great success in the Superbike World Championship and was raced through the 2007 season, despite no longer being produced.

STATS & FACTS

LAUNCHED: 2006

ORIGIN: ITALY

ENGINE: 61 CU IN (998 CC)

CYLINDERS: 2

MAXIMUM POWER: 143 BHP AT 10,000 RPM

MAXIMUM TORQUE: 82.5 LB PER SQ FT (111.8 NM) AT 8,000 RPM

GEARS: 6

DRY WEIGHT: 410 LB (186 KG)

MAX SPEED: 175 MPH (281.6 KM/H)

FUEL TANK CAPACITY: 4.1 GALLONS (15.5 LITERS)

COLORS: RED OR BLACK

COST: $30,986

Yamaha YZF R1

Originally a maker of musical instruments, Yamaha started making motorcycles after World War II. In 2009, Yamaha produced a new version of its open-class sports bike, the YZF-R1. The engine technology came from the M1 Moto GP bike driven by Valentino Rossi, with its cross-plane crankshaft and irregular firing intervals.

DID YOU KNOW?

A new throttle control allows the rider to choose between three distinct modes, depending on the rider's environment.

A subframe in magnesium cast in a carbon fiber mold makes the bike both strong and light.

In previous models the dual projector headlights were integrated with the air induction intakes. This accentuated the aerodynamic look and gave the bike an aggressive image.

STATS & FACTS

LAUNCHED: 2002

ORIGIN: JAPAN

ENGINE: 60.8 CU IN (998 CC)

CYLINDERS: 4

MAXIMUM POWER: 179 BHP AT 12,500 RPM

MAXIMUM TORQUE: 85 LB PER SQ FT (115.5 NM) AT 10,000 RPM

GEARS: 6

DRY WEIGHT: 454 LB (206 KG)

MAXIMUM SPEED: 182 MPH (293 KM/H)

FUEL TANK CAPACITY: 4.8 GALLONS (18 LITERS)

COLORS: CADMIUM YELLOW, RAVEN/CANDY RED, PEARL WHITE/ RAPID RED, TEAM YAMAHA BLUE/ WHITE

COST: $12,390

Honda CBR1100XX Blackbird

The Japanese company Honda wanted to design the fastest motorcycle ever. In 1996, it created the Blackbird, named after the Lockheed SR-71 aircraft, another record holder. With a few tweaks, the Blackbird could rocket to an incredible 200 mph (320 km/h). In 1999, Suzuki stole Honda's thunder with the Hayabusa (see pages 58–59).

DID YOU KNOW?

In 2001, a rider on a turbocharged Blackbird did a wheelie at an amazing 200 mph (320 km/h)!

The Blackbird had linked brakes. When the rider pulled the front brake lever, the back brake worked, too. The back brake pedal also controlled the front brake pedal.

The Honda CBR900RR Fireblade was smaller, lighter, and faster than the Blackbird. It could go from 0 to 100 mph (160 km/h) in six seconds.

STATS & FACTS

LAUNCHED: 1996

ORIGIN: JAPAN

ENGINE: 69.4 CU IN (1,137 CC)

CYLINDERS: 4

MAXIMUM POWER: 2.4 LB PER SQ FT (116 NM) AT 9,200 RPM

MAXIMUM TORQUE: 116 NM AT 7,300 RPM

GEARS: 6

DRY WEIGHT: 492 LB (223 KG)

MAXIMUM SPEED: 200 MPH (320 KM/H)

FUEL TANK CAPACITY: 6.3 GALLONS (24 LITERS)

COLORS: BLACK, BLUE, RED

COST: $16,687

Thanks to its streamlined shape and huge engine, this bike could race from 0 to 130 mph (209 km/h) in 11 seconds.

Aprilia RSV Mille R

The Italian company Aprilia first became known as a maker of bicycles. In 1968, it began producing motorcycles and mopeds. In 2002, Aprilia launched the Mille R. This beautiful machine was big, fast, and very comfortable. The *R* stands for "racing," since this bike was the fastest machine Aprilia ever made.

DID YOU KNOW?

Mille means "one thousand" in Italian. The RSV was called Mille because the engine was almost 1,000 cc.

Until 2001, all Mille Rs were single-seat bikes. In 2002, Aprilia made a two-seater version.

One of the most eye-catching features of the Aprilia was its triple headlight.

The Mille had special radial brakes at the front. These were extrastrong, so the bike could stop very quickly.

STATS & FACTS

LAUNCHED: 2002

ORIGIN: ITALY

ENGINE: 60.9 CU IN (997.6 CC)

CYLINDERS: 2

MAXIMUM POWER: 128 BHP AT 9,500 RPM

MAXIMUM TORQUE: 2.1 LB PER SQ FT (101 NM) AT 7,400 RPM

GEARS: 6

DRY WEIGHT: 370.4 LB (168 KG)

MAXIMUM SPEED: 168 MPH (270.4 KM/H)

FUEL TANK CAPACITY: 4.8 GALLONS (18 LITERS)

COLORS: APRILIA BLACK OR FLASHY YELLOW

COST: $16,125

Triumph Daytona 955i

The Triumph Daytona 955i is a sports bike manufactured by Triumph from 1997 to 2006. It was powered by a 955 cc liquid-cooled, 3-cylinder, 4-stroke engine. The bike was launched in 1997 as the Triumph T595 Daytona and renamed Triumph Daytona 955i in 1999.

The Triumph was powerful, but also heavy. It weighed 44 lb (20 kg) more than the Honda Fireblade.

DID YOU KNOW?

A Daytona was featured in *Mission Impossible 2*, which starred Tom Cruise.

This is the Triumph Speed-Twin. It was first made in 1937 and continued to be made for over 20 years.

The Daytona had a "naked" brother called the Speed Triple. It had the same engine and chassis, but no fairing.

STATS & FACTS

LAUNCHED: 1997

ORIGIN: UK

ENGINE: 58.3 CU IN (955 CC)

CYLINDERS: 3

MAXIMUM POWER: 147 BHP AT 10,700 RPM

MAXIMUM TORQUE: 2.1 LB PER SQ FT (100 NM) AT 8,200 RPM

GEARS: 6

DRY WEIGHT: 421 LB (191 KG)

MAXIMUM SPEED: 165 MPH (265.5 KM/H)

FUEL TANK CAPACITY: 5.5 GALLONS (21 LITERS)

COLORS: JET BLACK, ACIDIC YELLOW, TORNADO RED

COST: $14,130

On the Water

Meet the record holders of the sea, in all shapes and forms, from the massive *Stena Discovery* which can ferry 1,500 passengers and almost 400 cars at great speed thanks to its four gas turbine engines, to the superfast California Quake Drag Boat, the first racing boat to achieve ¼ mile in under five seconds. No less impressive is *Illbruck Challenge*, which sails around the globe battling waves, howling gales, and collisions with icebergs and whales, powered only by the wind and the sheer determination of its crew.

Yamaha FZR WaveRunner

A combination of motorcycle, water ski, and snowmobile, the WaveRunner can surge across waves at great speeds. It was the first sit-down watercraft designed for stand-up riding.

Thanks to nanotechnology, the WaveRunner has stronger hulls, decks, and liners that are 25 percent lighter than previous models.

DID YOU KNOW?
The telescopic steering column makes it easy for riders to go from sitting to standing, with three different riding positions.

DID YOU KNOW?

Yet more unusual facts are bound to surprise you. Who would have thought that the nuclear-powered Nimitz-class Aircraft Carrier could go 20 years without refueling and last for 50 years? And there's more...

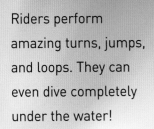

Riders perform amazing turns, jumps, and loops. They can even dive completely under the water!

STATS & FACTS

All key data at your fingertips, to help you compare engine, size, weight, and speed of the kings of the sea. Get on board and test the water!

The keel shape is designed for high-speed, supertight turning. Large pump inlets ducts provide great pickup.

STATS & FACTS

LAUNCHED: 2009

ORIGIN: US

ENGINE: 4-CYLINDER, 4-STROKE

LENGTH: 132¾ IN (3.4 M)

WIDTH: 48½ IN (1.23 M)

SPEED: 0–30 MPH (50 KM) IN 1.7 SECONDS

MAXIMUM WEIGHT: 353 LB (160 KG)

LOAD: 2 RIDERS

FUEL CAPACITY: 18.5 GALLONS (70 LITERS)

COST: $12,599

83

California Quake Drag Boat

The fastest racing boats on the water are drag boats. These single-seater crafts surge like rockets at breathtaking speeds over the waves, often spending more time above the surface than on it.

Thanks to the 5,000 hp engine, this drag boat became the first to achieve ¼ mile in under five seconds—a world record!

Bottled air is supplied to the driver's helmet. If the driver crashes, he can still breathe while waiting for divers to rescue him.

DID YOU KNOW?

This model has reached speeds of 230 mph (370 km/h).

The safety capsule breaks free from the boat in the event of a high-speed crash.

STATS & FACTS

LAUNCHED: 1999

ORIGIN: US

ENGINES: 500 CUBIC INCH NITROMETHANE ENGINE GENERATING 5,000 HP

LENGTH: 25 FT (7.62 M)

WIDTH: 12 FT 3 IN (3.72 M)

MAXIMUM SPEED: 198 KNOTS (230 MPH/370 KM/H)

MAXIMUM WEIGHT: 5.25 TONS (4.75 METRIC TONS)

LOAD: 1 PILOT

FUEL CAPACITY: 5.3 GALLONS (20 LITERS)

COST: $100,000

Stena Discovery HSS Ferry

Stena HSS (High-speed Sea Service) ferries are high-speed car carriers. They are catamarans, which means they have two hulls instead of one. The design makes for a smooth, speedy ride.

DID YOU KNOW?

Most car ferries are "Ro-Ro"— roll (drive) on and roll (drive) off. In the past, cranes lifted each car on and off the boats.

The hulls are made from aluminum, which is light and does not rust.

Ferries operate worldwide. This one serves the Caribbean and can hold 200 cars and 1,000 passengers. It has lounge areas where passengers can relax during the crossing.

Four massive gas turbine engines produce as much power as 600 car engines.

STATS & FACTS

LAUNCHED: 1997

ORIGIN: FINLAND

ENGINES: 2 GE LM2500 GAS TURBINES, GENERATING 20,500 KW (27,490 HP) EACH, AND 2 GE LM1600 GAS TURBINES, PRODUCING 13,500 KW (18,103 HP) EACH

LENGTH: 415 FT (126.5 M)

WIDTH: 131 FT (40 M)

MAXIMUM SPEED: 40 KNOTS (46 MPH/74 KM/H)

MAXIMUM WEIGHT: 1,650 TONS (1,500 METRIC TONS)

LOAD: 1,500 PASSENGERS AND 375 CARS

FUEL CAPACITY: 2,642 GALLONS (10,000 LITERS)

COST: $100 MILLION

Illbruck Racing Yacht

Inspired by the Whitbread Round the World Race and called the "Everest of sailing," the Volvo Ocean Race has taken place every three years since 2001. The nine-month race covers 37,000 miles (59,500 km). The first winner was *Illbruck Challenge*.

Crews pull the cables for the sails using high-speed winches with long handles. The tallest mast is 85 ft (26 m).

DID YOU KNOW?

The original race was inspired by the great seafarers who sailed the world's oceans aboard square-rigged clipper ships more than a century ago.

Round-the-world yachts battle giant waves, howling gales, collisions with icebergs and whales—and each other!

The satellite communications center contains telephone, email, and video transmission facilities.

STATS & FACTS

LAUNCHED: 2001

ORIGIN: GERMANY

ENGINES: N/A

LENGTH: 64 FT (19.5 M)

WIDTH: 17 FT (5.25 M)

MAXIMUM SPEED: 36.75 KNOTS (42 MPH/67.6 KM/H)

MAXIMUM WEIGHT: 14.9 TONS (13.5 METRIC TONS)

LOAD: 12 PEOPLE

COST: $24 MILLION

Atlantic 75 Lifeboat

The Atlantic 75 is a Rigid Inflatable Lifeboat (RIB) used to rescue people in trouble up to 50 miles (80 km) out to sea. It has a glass-reinforced plastic hull topped by an inflatable tube called a sponson. The latest version of this boat is the Atlantic 85 Lifeboat.

The hull and sponson are divided into compartments. If one section is pierced, the boat will not sink.

DID YOU KNOW?

If the boat capsizes, the crew inflates an airbag. The boat then turns the right way up in seconds.

The first rigid-hull inflatable lifeboat was designed by the British-based Royal National Lifeboat Institution in the early 1960s. These boats are now used worldwide.

The outboard motors are immersion-proofed so if the boat capsizes they are not damaged.

STATS & FACTS

LAUNCHED: 1992

ORIGIN: UK

MAXIMUM POWER: 2 X 70 BHP

LENGTH: 25 FT (7.5 M)

HEIGHT: 20 IN (50 CM)

MAXIMUM SPEED: 32 KNOTS (37 MPH/60 KM/H)

FUEL CAPACITY: 48 GALLONS (181 LITERS)

MAXIMUM LOAD: 1,100 LB (500 KG)

WEIGHT: 1.5 TONS (1.4 METRIC TONS)

ENDURANCE: 3 HOURS AT MAXIMUM SPEED

CREW: 3-PERSON

Nimitz-Class Aircraft Carrier

Nimitz-class aircraft carriers are the biggest warships ever built. Each of these giants is a floating army, navy, and air force. The crew is the size of a small town: 3,360 ship's crew and 2,500 air crew, not including soldiers and pilots!

The supercarrier holds up to 85 planes and six helicopters, along with their crew and supplies. Jet fuel is stored in swimming-pool-sized tanks.

DID YOU KNOW?

These nuclear-powered ships can go 20 years without refueling and have a life span of 50 years.

Supercarriers are equipped with the latest computers, radar, and missiles. It takes three years to refuel, re-equip, and refit these monsters.

STATS & FACTS

LAUNCHED: 1972

ORIGIN: US

ENGINES: 2 NUCLEAR ENGINES POWERING 4 STEAM TURBINES PRODUCING 260,000 HP

LENGTH: 1,093 FT (333 M)

WIDTH: 134 FT (40.8 M)

MAXIMUM SPEED: MORE THAN 30 KNOTS (35 MPH/56 KM/H)

MAXIMUM WEIGHT: 100,000 TONS (90,718 METRIC TONS)

LOAD: 3,360 SHIP'S COMPANY AND 2,500 AIR CREW

COST: $4.5 BILLION

The Nimitz-class supercarrier is almost as long as the Empire State Building is tall.

Yamaha FZR WaveRunner

A combination of motorcycle, water ski, and snowmobile, the WaveRunner can surge across waves at great speeds. It was the first sit-down watercraft designed for stand-up riding.

Thanks to nanotechnology, the WaveRunner has stronger hulls, decks, and liners that are 25 percent lighter than previous models.

DID YOU KNOW?

The telescopic steering column makes it easy for riders to go from sitting to standing, with three different riding positions.

Riders perform amazing turns, jumps, and loops. They can even dive completely under the water!

The keel shape is designed for high-speed, supertight turning. Large pump inlets ducts provide great pickup.

STATS & FACTS

LAUNCHED: 2009

ORIGIN: US

ENGINE: 4-CYLINDER, 4-STROKE

LENGTH: 132¾ IN (3.4 M)

WIDTH: 48½ IN (1.23 M)

SPEED: 0–30 MPH (50 KM) IN 1.7 SECONDS

MAXIMUM WEIGHT: 353 LB (160 KG)

LOAD: 2 RIDERS

FUEL CAPACITY: 18.5 GALLONS (70 LITERS)

COST: $12,599

Fire Dart Fireboat

The Fire Dart is a firefighting boat that patrols the Thames River in London. It is one of the lightest and quickest fireboats ever built.

DID YOU KNOW?

The Fire Dart can stop in about 46 feet (14 meters).

Two massive engines provide more than 700 bhp!

Fireboats and firefighting tugboats tackle fires on board ships. There is never a danger that they will run out of water because they take their water from the river or sea.

A jet called a deck monitor shoots water in a stream over a fire. The rescue boat releases 475 gallons (1,800 liters) per minute.

OWNER No 3081   REG No 4768

STATS & FACTS

LAUNCHED: 1999

ORIGIN: UK

MAXIMUM POWER: 2 X 365 BHP

LENGTH: 46 FT (14.10 M)

WIDTH: 14 FT (4.2 M)

HEIGHT: 10 FT (3 M)

MAXIMUM SPEED: 30 KNOTS (35 MPH/56 KM/H)

FUEL CAPACITY: 1,057 GALLONS (4,000 LITERS)

MAXIMUM LOAD: 1.3 TONS (1.2 METRIC TONS)

WEIGHT: 6.7 TONS (6.1 METRIC TONS)

RANGE: 100 MILES (160 KM)

CREW: 4 CREW, PLUS 5 FIREFIGHTERS

Trent-Type Lifeboat

Every sailor fears shipwreck and drowning at sea. Brave lifeboat crews are always ready for rescue missions, even in the worst storms. Powerful Trent-Type lifeboats are run by Britain's RNLI (Royal National Lifeboat Institution).

The survivor's cabin holds ten people. On board there are also heaters, dry clothes, and a small galley.

DID YOU KNOW?

Two hundred and thirty RNLI stations in Great Britain and Ireland provide coverage 50 miles (80 km) out to sea.

Radar and radio equipment tracks ships in distress using the Marsat and Sarsat emergency satellite navigation systems.

The hull is made of plastics, carbon fiber, and composites. These materials are light, strong, and never rust.

STATS & FACTS

LAUNCHED: 1994

ORIGIN: UNITED KINGDOM

ENGINES: 2-MAN DIESELS, 808 HP PER ENGINE, EACH ABOUT AS POWERFUL AS A FORMULA 1 RACE CAR ENGINE

LENGTH: 47 FT (14.26 M)

MAXIMUM SPEED: 25 KNOTS (29 MPH/47 KM/H)

MAXIMUM WEIGHT: 30 TONS (27.5 METRIC TONS)

LOAD: 6 CREW, PLUS 10 SURVIVORS

FUEL CAPACITY: 1,000 GALLONS (4,100 LITERS)

COST: $1.9 MILLION

Marine Protector

This is a Marine Protector Class Coast Guard patrol boat. It is a fast, strong boat that can operate in rough seas. It is used to stop drug smugglers and chase other criminals. It is also used for search and rescue missions.

The pilot house is equipped with satellite navigation and autopilot.

DID YOU KNOW?

Each of the 73 boats in the Coast Guard fleet is named after a marine predator. Names include *Marlin*, *Stingray*, and *Mako*.

U.S. COAST GUARD

A small diesel-powered boat is kept at the back of the patrol boat. It is launched and recovered on a specially designed ramp. Only one person is required on deck for launch and recovery.

This boat is called a cutter. Cutters are boats that are more than 65 feet (20 meters) long.

STATS & FACTS

LAUNCHED: 1998

ORIGIN: US

MAXIMUM POWER: 5,360 BHP

LENGTH: 87 FT (26.5 M)

WIDTH: 17 FT (5.18 M)

MAXIMUM SPEED: 25 KNOTS (28 MPH/45 KM/H)

FUEL CAPACITY: 29,000 GALLONS (11,000 LITERS)

MAXIMUM WEIGHT: 102 TONS (92.4 METRIC TONS)

TOWING CAPABILITY: 220 TONS (200 METRIC TONS)

SURVIVOR CAPACITY: 10

RANGE: 900 MILES (1,445 KM)

ENDURANCE: 5 DAYS

CREW: 10-PERSON

DeepFlight Submersible

Submersibles are miniature submarines used for deep-sea exploration. DeepFlight is a tiny one-person submersible with short wings that allow it to "fly" through the water.

Lightweight material is strong enough to resist the tremendous pressure of the deep.

DID YOU KNOW?

In 2012, filmmaker and ocean explorer James Cameron reached the deepest point in the ocean—the Mariana Trench—in a custom-built one-man submersible. He descended almost 7 miles (11 km).

A submersible has the layout of a plane. Unlike a plane, however, the stubby wings pull the craft down through the water, rather than up off the ground.

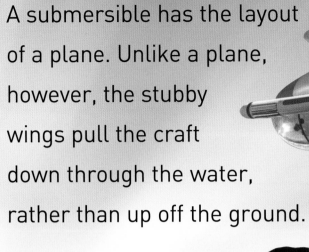

DeepFlight is equipped with six lights, which are needed because the bottom of the ocean is totally dark.

STATS & FACTS

LAUNCHED: 1996

ORIGIN: US

ENGINES: 2 MOTORS POWERED BY 10 12-VOLT, LEAD-ACID BATTERIES, GENERATING 5 HP EACH

LENGTH: 13 FT (4 M)

WIDTH: 8 FT (2.4 M)

MAXIMUM SPEED: 12 KNOTS (13.8 MPH/22.2 KM/H)

MAXIMUM WEIGHT: 1.4 TONS (1.3 METRIC TONS)

ASCENT RATE: 650 FT (198 M) PER MINUTE

DESCENT RATE: 480 FT (150 M) PER MINUTE

MAXIMUM DEPTH: NEWER DEEPFLIGHT CHALLENGER WILL REACH 37,000 FT (11 KM)

LOAD: 1 PILOT

COST: $1.5 MILLION (IN 2009)

Glossary

ACCELERATION The act of making a vehicle go faster using the accelerator pedal.

AERODYNAMIC A shape that cuts through the air around it.

AFTERBURNER System that injects extra fuel into the exhaust gases of a plane to provide large amounts of extra power.

AIR REFUELING Method of refueling military aircraft while in flight, via a fuel hose linked to a tanker aircraft.

ALUMINUM A lightweight, strong metal that does not rust.

AUTOPILOT System that operates a vehicle without a pilot.

BHP Brake horse power, the measure of an engine's power output.

BODY Main part of a vehicle that houses the driver and passengers.

BOOSTERS Large canisters containing fuel that are attached to the sides of a space rocket as it is launched.

BRAKES Part of a vehicle used to slow it down.

CABIN A room in a ship used as living quarters by an officer or passenger, or the part of a plane that houses the crew and passengers.

CAPSIZE When a boat turns over in the water.

CARBON/GLASS FIBER A modern strong, but lightweight, material.

CATAMARAN A boat or ship with two hulls that are joined together by a wide deck or decks over the top.

CC Cubic capacity, the measurement used for the size of an engine.

CHASSIS The part that holds the engine, wheels, and body together.

COCKPIT The part of an aircraft for the pilot and assistants.

COMPOSITE A material or substance that is made of a mixture of materials, such as plastic, metal, and fiberglass. Composites are usually very light and strong.

CUTTER A boat more than 65 feet (20 meters) long.

CYLINDER The part of an engine where fuel is burned to make energy.

DECK MONITOR Water jet on a fireboat that shoots water high into the air.

DECKS The main floors or stories of a ship and especially the uppermost flat area where people walk.

EJECTION SEAT A seat, usually installed in military aircraft, that can be fired or ejected from the aircraft.

ENGINE The part of a plane where fuel is burned to create energy.

EXHAUST Pipe at the back of a motor vehicle that lets out poisonous gases made when fuel is burned. In some cases it is also used to reduce engine noise.

FAIRING Part of a bike covering the engine, whose function is to produce a smooth outline so the motorcyle goes faster.

FIRE RETARDANT Liquid dropped onto fires to stop them from spreading.

FOREPLANES Movable surfaces at the front of a plane that provide extra lift and balance.

FORMULA ONE Famous car racing championship.

FOUR-WHEEL DRIVE A car that has power delivered to all four wheels.

FRAME The part of a bike that holds the engine, wheels, and bodywork together. Also called the chassis.

FUSELAGE *See* Cabin.

GEARS System that lets a vehicle change speed without harming the engine.

GEAR-SHIFT PADDLES Levers on a steering wheel used to shift gears up and down.

HEADLIGHT The bright light at the front of a bike or car.

HORSEPOWER (HP) The measure of an engine's power, originally based on the power of an engine compared to a horse.

HULL The lower part of a boat or ship.

HYPERSONIC Able to reach speeds of Mach 5 and above.

IMMERSION-PROOFED Protected from water damage.

INFLATABLE A small rubber boat or raft filled with air.

JET Stream of fluid forced out under pressure from a narrow opening or nozzle.

JETS Part of an engine that provides the lifting power for an aircraft.

KNOT One nautical mile per hour, equal to 1.15 miles per hour or 1.85 kilometers per hour.

LASER-GUIDED BOMB A bomb launched from an aircraft, which has sensors in its nose to guide it onto a target.

LINKED BRAKES System where the front brake lever also works the back brake, and the back brake lever works the front brake.

MACH Measurement that relates the speed of an aircraft to the speed of sound. Mach 1 is the speed of sound; Mach 2 is twice the speed of sound.

MAST A tall pole on a ship that may hold up sails, radio antennas, radar dishes, or even flags.

MONITOR A mounted water cannon that throws powerful jets of water at a fire.

NANOTECHNOLOGY The science of using materials on a molecular scale, especially to create microscopic devices.

NOSE The rounded front of an aircraft or the front end of a car.

NOZZLE The end of a hose. Different nozzle attachments result in different water sprays, from a mist to a continuous stream.

ORBITER A spacecraft or satellite designed to orbit a planet or other body without landing on it.

PARACHUTE A large canopy with a body harness underneath. It is designed to slow the rate of descent of a person from an aircraft.

PILOT A person qualified to fly an aircraft or spaceship.

PILOT HOUSE Part of a ship where the pilot and the controls are based.

PROPELLER A machine with spinning blades that provides thrust to lift an aircraft.

PUMP A machine that raises or lifts a liquid or gas.

RADAR A method of detecting distant objects using radio waves.

RADIAL BRAKES Braking system where the brake discs are mounted at the bottom of the forks, parallel to the wheel.

RIGGED A ship equipped with sails and the ropes and chains used to control them.

RIGID HULL INFLATABLE BOAT Boat with a plastic hull topped by an inflatable tube called a sponson.

ROLL CAGE A metal framework in a car or racing boat to limit the damage if it turns over in an accident.

ROTOR Spinning blade.

RPM Revolutions (revs) of an engine per minute.

SAILS Fabric spread to catch or deflect the wind as a means of propelling a ship or boat.

SATELLITE NAVIGATION A system that tells you where you are and gives you directions by using satellites in space.

SCRAMJET A hydrogen-fueled engine designed for flying at five times the speed of sound.

SENSORS Devices that help pilots fly their aircraft, detect enemy aircraft, or fire weapons accurately.

SPOILER A lightweight panel attached to a car to prevent the vehicle from lifting up at high speeds.

SPONSON An air-filled tube that helps stabilize a boat on the water.

SPORTS BIKE A fast motorcycle that has been developed for road use.

STEALTH TECHNOLOGY Technology used to make a plane almost invisible.

STEEL Very strong alloy usually made by combining iron with carbon.

SUBMARINE *See* submersible.

SUBMERSIBLE A boat that can function under water.

SUBSONIC Slower than the speed of sound.

SUPERBIKE A fast motorcycle that is very similar to a racing motorcycle.

SUPERCAR A high-performance, high-cost production car.

SUPERSONIC Faster than the speed of sound.

SUSPENSION Springs and shock absorbers attached to a vehicle's wheels, intended to ensure a smooth ride even when travelling on bumpy surfaces.

TAIL The rear of a car or the rear part of the fuselage that balances a plane.

TANK A large container used to store fuel.

THROTTLE The part of a bike that is used to make it go faster or slower.

THRUST A pushing force created in a jet engine or rocket that gives aircraft enough speed to take off.

TIRE A rubber covering for a wheel, filled with compressed air.

TITANIUM ALLOY A light, strong, and heat-tolerant material.

TORQUE AND NM The measurements for an engine's power.

TUG A powerful boat that pulls or pushes ships.

TURBINE Machine with a wheel or rotor driven by water, steam, or gases.

TURBO System that increases a motor vehicle's power by forcing more air into the engine.

TURBOFAN An engine with a fan used to boost its power.

V/INLINE/FLAT The arrangement of the cylinders in an engine.

V8/V12 The engine size given in number of cylinders.

VALVE Device that controls the flow of fuel into an engine.

VIFF Vectoring in Forward Flight. A system that lets a plane change direction very suddenly.

VTOL Vertical Take-off, Vertical Landing. System that holds an aircraft in the air as it takes off or lands.

WINCH The method of lifting something by winding a line around a spool.

WINGS Part of an aircraft that provides lift, placed on each side of the fuselage.

WINGSPAN The distance between the tips of the wings of an aircraft.

Index

Index